Soft and White

Guyla Nelson

and

Saundra Scovell Lamgo

Illustrated by David Grassnick

American Language Series™
A Silent E Reader

MILE-HI
PUBLISHERS™

Distributed under license by
Lighthouse Publishers, LLC
PO Box 570
Greer, SC 29652
www.lighthousepublishers.com

ISBN-13 978-1-934470-07-7
ISBN-10 1-934470-07-4

Printed in China

For all boys and girls
who wish to
become readers of
good books —
and especially the
Book of Books, the Bible

Stories

	Page
What Is My Name?	1
Things in the Sky	2
The Safe	3
A Can of Sage	4
A Snake Made of Grass	6
The Cake	8
Dave	10
Who Wins the Race?	12
My Best Theme	14
Eve Is Here	15
The Scheme	16
A Spring Scene	18
Squire! Squire!	20
Smile	21

Mike's Bike 22

I Will Not Whine! 23

My Kite 25

A Nice Place 26

The Canes 27

Lots of Flakes 28

Soft and White 29

The Chip Dip 30

Five Mice 31

Slice the Cake! 32

The Lame Man 34

The Flat Tire 36

My Flag Waves 38

My Nice Mom 39

Smile in the Sun 40

The Plane Trip 42

Spring Is Here 44

My Bone 46

The Cup 47

A Wild Mole 48

Wild Rose Buds 50

The Old Lamp 51

A Ship in the Cove 52

Tate and Kate 54

The Tam 56

The Man in the Cave 58

A Case of Eggs 60

Eve's Robe 62

Skate on the Lake 64

What Lot Chose 66

Mom's Jade Ring 67

A Vase of Buds 68

Who Is This Man? 69

The Pink Dress 70

The Sun 71

A Lone Cat 72

A Bronze Frame 74

A Big Job 75

Fix-Up Time 76

What Is the Gift? 78

My Note 80

The Scribe 82

Ten Dimes 84

On the Line 86

Dale on His Trike 89

It Is a Gift! 92

A Trip to the Store 94

A Close Race 96

The Class 98

Five in a Hive 100

A Truce! A Truce! 101

A Huge Black Mule 102

A Cube 103

The Tunes 104

Fun on a Tube 106

A Hole in a Sole 108

Bruce on a Mule 109

The Huge Whale 110

A Stitch in Time Saves Nine! 112

The Cold Drink 114

The Tale of the Fox 116

Wade's Ice Cubes 118

The Pane 120

Watch Luke! 121

The Cute Pup 123

The Ninth Grade 124

The Yule Log 126

Steve 128

The Bride 130

The Lime Drink 131

A Trip to the Lake 132

The Ox and His Mate 134

Jake Will Make a Lake 136

Quite a Sight! 138

Help! Help! 140

Frank's Lunch 142

Rice and Grapes 144

A Nice Ride 146

The Ape 149

Five Rules 150

What Time Is It? 152

Can We Find the Sum? 154

Which Size Is Best? 157

Bruce Has Six Rules 159

The Kites 161

The Dike 164

Whose Glove Is This? 168

Sage

Pace

Chase

Case

Tate

Hale

Kate

Page

Gage

Blaze

Jake

Dane

What Is My Name?

Dale

What is my name?
What is my name?
Print it and spell it—
It is just the same.

Dave

Thane

Gale

Blake

James

Jane

Lane

Drake

Shane

Grace

Crane

1

Wade

Zale

Kate

Things in the Sky

Dale thinks it is fun to gaze at the sky.

He spots lots of things that God has made.

Let us help Dale name the things in the sky that God has made.

The Safe

Dad will place his cash in the safe.

He will stack the cash on the top shelf.

Then he will lock the safe.

The cash will not be lost in the safe.

Dad's cash will be safe.

A Can of Sage

Mom will stuff the wild game.

She will take a can of sage from the shelf.

She will shake the sage flakes on the wild duck.

The sage will make the wild game taste swell.

A Snake Made of Grass

Wade and Jake will rest in the shade.

It will not be hot in the shade.

Wade will snip blades of grass.

He will twist the blades of grass to make a snake.

The snake will be as long as his leg.

Wade and Jake think it is fun to rest in the shade and make grass snakes.

The Cake

Mom will bake a cake.

She will set it on a plate.

Then she will frost it.

Next she will make pink buds.

She will trim the cake with the
pink buds.

Dad and James watch Mom cut
the cake.

Dad thinks the cake with the pink
buds tastes swell.

Dave

Dave will rake the grass.

He will rake and rake.

Then he will put the grass, the twigs, and a big branch by the path.

Next he will find ten tan bags.

He will fill the bags with the grass, the twigs, and the branch.

Dave will fling the bags into the back of the truck.

Then Dad will take the bags and dump them.

Who Wins the Race?

Bill and Sam plan to have a race up the lane.

Bill is set to run.

Sam is set to run.

Bill waves to Sam.

Sam waves to Bill.

Off the lads go!

Bill runs fast.

Sam runs fast.

Sam runs past Bill.

Sam wins the race.

Then he stands and waves at Bill till
Bill gets to the end of the race.

My Best Theme

Here is my scheme
And here is my plan—
To print my best theme
As fast as I can!

Eve Is Here

Knock! Knock! Knock!

Eve is here at my home. She is my pal.

I think Eve has a gift.

Will it be a game?

We will have fun while she is here.

I am glad when Eve comes to my home.

The Scheme

Pete has a scheme.

He plans to trick his pal, Brad.

When Brad gets here, then Pete will trick him.

He will hand Brad a big box.

Brad will think a gift is in the big box.

When Brad lifts the lid, a pink and red
flag will pop up.

Pete thinks his scheme is swell.

It will be fun to trick Brad.

Pete will be glad when his pal gets here.

A Spring Scene

My name is Brent.

My age is six.

I will sketch a scene.

The theme of my sketch will be spring.

I will sketch a tame drake on the lake.

A drake is a male duck.

Then I will make blades of grass next to the lake.

I will sketch a snake in the grass.

I will place the sun in the sky.

I will frame my spring scene and hang it on the wall.

Squire! Squire!

Squire, Squire!

My case is dire!

The old worn tire

Just fell in the mire!

What! fell in the mire!

Just hold the ire.

My roll of wire

Will save that tire!

Smile

Smile, smile, smile.

I like to smile.

I will smile when I am sad.

I will smile when I am glad.

Smile, smile, smile.

I like to smile.

Mike's Bike

Mike likes his bike.

It is white with red stripes.

It shines in the sun.

When the trim on Mike's bike gets a spot on it, he wipes it with a white rag.

He rubs and shines the trim.

Mike's bike is just his size.

He will ride it five miles with Dad.

I Will Not Whine!

It is not nice to whine.

When I whine, Mom is sad.

When I whine, Dad is sad.

And when I whine, God is sad.

I must not whine, but I must smile and
be kind.

Then I will be glad.

Then Mom and Dad will be glad.

Then God will be glad.

I will not whine!

My Kite

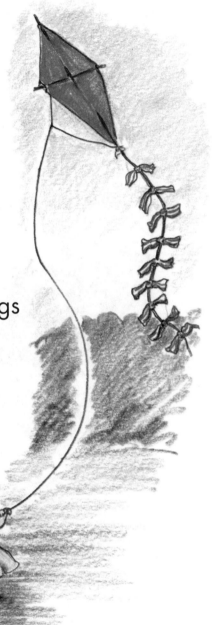

My kite glides and
slides in the sky.

The wind sends my kite
up and up.

I have a white line
on my kite.

On the line I put nine rags
with red and white stripes.

The rags must not
be wide in size.

My kite makes me
smile and smile
to watch it
in the sky.

A Nice Place

We will skip up the lane.

We will go to a nice place.

This place is in the shade.

We will wade at this nice place.

Can we tell the name of this
nice place?

This nice place is a lake.

The Canes

Zeke will make a red and white cane.

He will tape his cane by the fire.

Gale made a cane.

It is a pink cane.

Gale's cane will hang next to Zeke's cane.

Lots of Flakes

I will fill my dish with lots of flakes.

Then I will put milk on the flakes.

The flakes taste fine.

I will munch on a roll and jam.

Then I will place my dish and knife

in the sink.

Soft and White

The lamb is soft and white.

He is not big yet.

The lamb likes to romp and romp on the grass.

At lunch time he stops to graze on the grass.

The grass makes a fine lunch.

God made the soft, white lamb.

The Chip Dip

Mom will fix a fine chip dip.

She will mix chives in the dip.

The dip will taste fine.

She will place the chips on a plate
and the dip in a dish.

We will have the chips and dip at
snack time.

Five Mice

Five mice will munch on the cake.

Then the mice will munch on the rolls.

Then the mice will taste the rice and the nuts.

Mom will not like the big mess that the mice made.

Slice the Cake!

Mom will put the spice cake on a cake plate.

Then she will slice the spice cake with a knife.

She will cut the cake nine times.

Abe will take a big bite of his slice.

"The spice cake tastes fine!" he tells Mom.

He plans to munch on lots of cake.

Mom tells Abe to rest a while.

He must not munch so much cake that he gets sick!

The Lame Man

The lame man is sad.

He cannot run.

He cannot jump.

He must sit and rest on his mat.

A kind Man came by.

He told the lame man to rise.

Will the lame man stand up?

Yes. He will do as the kind Man tells him.

He can stand. He is not lame.

The Man made the lame man well.

Tell the name of the kind Man.

The Flat Tire

Pssshhh! The tire is flat!

Dad is sad.

He must change the tire.

Mom and Jan will not sit in the van.

Dad will jack up the back of the van.

Then he will take the tire off.

He will fix the flat tire.

It will not take long.

Then Dad, Mom, and Jan will go to the lake.

My Flag Waves

My flag waves in the wind.
The sun shines
on my flag.
It makes me
glad as my
flag waves
in the wind.
I like my flag.
My flag is a
grand flag.
This is the
flag of my land.

My Nice Mom

Mom will make me a white dress.

The dress will be full.

Then Mom will make the same dress from tan silk.

It will have a cape on top.

I will save my tan dress till spring.

Mom thinks my tan dress is just fine.

I like it!

Smile in the Sun

God makes the sun to shine.

When it shines on me, it makes me smile.

I like to let the sun shine on my face.

I like to run and jump in the sun.

I like to sit and rest in the sun.

The sun makes me hot.

I must stop and rest in the shade.

I am glad God made the sun to shine.

Thanks, God, that the sun shines on me.

The Plane Trip

Dad will go on a trip.

He will go on a plane.

Dad is late.

He must not miss the plane.

Dad must run to catch the plane.

He runs and runs.

He runs fast.

Dad has a case in his hand.

Will he make it to the plane in time?

Yes, he will.

Dad just made it.

He just made it in time to get on the plane.

Dad will have a nice ride on the plane.

Spring Is Here!

Spring is here!

I spy buds.

I spy buds on the vine.

I spy a big hive on the branch.

In spring the sun is bright.

It will shine and shine.

The sun will shine on my face.

I like spring.

I am glad spring is here.

I am glad God makes the spring time.

My Bone

My bone, my bone,
Who hid my bone?

Shall I lift the rug?
Shall I pull and tug?

My bone, my bone,
Who hid my bone?

The Cup

Hope Stone has a cup.

Crash!

Oh! Oh!

Hope's cup fell. It broke!

The cup fell from Hope's hands.

She hopes Dad can mend the cup.

But Dad cannot mend it. Why?

A Wild Mole

The mole will doze.

He will doze in his hole.

The hole is in a cave.

The hole is small.

The hole is the mole's home.

God made the mole.

The mole is not tame.

He is wild.

I will not pet the mole.

I will not wake him.

I will let the mole doze and get

his rest.

Wild Rose Buds

We will skip up the lane.

We will pick wild rose buds from a bush.

We must not let the bush stick us.

Then we will skip back on the lane and go home.

We will give Mom the wild rose buds.

She will cut the stems and then put them in a vase.

The Old Lamp

Mom had an old, old, glass lamp.

The glass lamp fell from the desk.

The glass lamp shade broke.

Nate will try to fix the shade.

He hopes he can mend it, since the lamp

was a gift to his mom.

A Ship in the Cove

The cove is close to the glade.

The ship will dock in the cove.

The men will get off the ship and go
to the glade.

The men will chop lots of logs and
then come back to the ship.

The men will bring the logs to
the ship with them.

The men will spend the night on the
ship in the cove.

Tate and Kate

Tate is Kate's twin.

Tate and Kate go to a cave.

Kate falls in a hole.

Tate runs to help Kate.

He gets a rope and flings the rope to Kate.

Kate grabs the rope and climbs up the rope.

Tate takes hold of Kate's hand.

He lifts Kate from the hole.

Kate is safe. Kate thanks Tate.

Then Kate and Tate rush from the cave.

The Tam

The lass has on a cape.

She has on a tam.

The cape and tam match.

The lass skips on the path.

The tam falls off while she skips.

The lass did not miss the tam till she got home.

Then she had to go back on the path to find the tam.

Did the lass find the tam?

Yes, she did find it.

The lass is glad she went back.

The Man in the Cave

The cave was in the vale.

The men slept in the cave.

The king slept in the cave.

The men hid from the king.

A man cut a hunk from the king's robe.

But the kind man did not kill the king.

Then the king woke up.

His robe was cut, but he was safe.

What is the name of the kind man?

What is the name of the king?

A Case of Eggs

We will set the case in a safe place.

Then Dan, Rose, and I will fill the case with fresh eggs. It will hold twelve flats of eggs.

We must not crack the eggs. When the case is full, Dan and I will close the lid and tape it shut. We will lift the case and place it in the back of the van.

We will take the case of eggs to Jake Crane. He will sell the fresh eggs in his store.

Eve's Robe

Eve woke up at six.

She had slept well.

When Eve got up, she chose to put on a pink robe.

Eve tore a hole in the robe.

Eve felt bad.

Mom will fix Eve's robe.

She will mend the hole.

Skate on the Lake

Jane and I will skate on the lake.

The wind is strong and cold.

It will snap at my nose and bite my hands.

The wind will make Jane cold, and it will make me cold.

We like to skate and we will not let the cold wind chase us from the lake. We will skate till five.

What Lot Chose

Lot chose the best land.

He set up his tents.

He let his lambs graze on the grass.

When Lot chose that land, it made God sad.

His life did not make God glad.

God did not bless Lot.

Mom's Jade Ring

Mom has a ring.

Dad gave the ring to Mom as a gift.

The ring is gold.

The gold ring has a jade stone set in it.

The jade stone has a shape like a rose.

Mom likes the jade ring.

A Vase of Buds

Jane is ill and must rest in bed.

Grace stands by the bed and hands Jane a nice vase of buds.

Jane likes the red rose, but she likes the white rose best.

Grace is kind to Jane.
Jane thanks Grace.

Who Is This Man?

A sad man sat next to the fire.

A lass spoke to the man, but he did not tell the truth.

Then thrice the cock made a cry.

The man went from the fire and wept.

Who is this man?

The Pink Dress

At the store Gale chose pink cloth and soft, white lace.

Mom will make a dress from the cloth.

The lace will go on the neck of the dress.

Mom will do a fine job on the pink dress.

The Sun

The sun rose up so bright at five.

God made the nice sun.

Thanks, God, that it shines on us.

At night the sun will not shine.

It will set in the West.

Then it will be night time.

A Lone Cat

A lone cat sat on the ledge.

He did not budge.

James has a pan of scraps.

He will try to tempt the lone cat from the ledge.

He will be kind to the cat.

The cat will munch on the scraps in the pan.

James will be glad.

James likes his nice pet.

A Bronze Frame

Clint Price has a made gift which he hands to Deb White.

Deb will take the gift to Mom.

The gift is a bronze frame.

Mom will hang the bronze frame next to Deb's bed.

She will tell Deb to write Clint a note of thanks.

A Big Job

Dad will drive his truck to the store.

He will pick up a hose, a big box of plants, a rake, and lots of wire.

Dad will get a rope, stakes, and six stone tiles.

What will Dad do with the things in his truck?

Fix-Up Time

Dad will fix the steps
at home.

Then he will plant grass.

He will plant shrubs and
a bush.

76

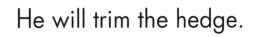He will trim the hedge.

Next he will fix the
gate so that it will close.

Then Dad will fix a lamp on
a pole by the path. The lamp
will shine on the path.
Dad will do a fine job.

What Is the Gift?

Tom gave Shane a gift.

Shane will set the gift on his desk.

Shane will try to find Rome with his gift.

Then he will find the Nile.

Next Shane will try to find the lake
on which he and Dad went to fish.

And then Shane will find his home on
the gift.

Shane thinks Tom's gift is nice.

Can we tell what the gift is?

The gift is a globe.

My Note

I wrote a note to Thane.

I did my best.

I wrote my note with pen and ink.

My note told Thane that I hope to find a game.

I will give the game to him.

The game will be my gift to him.

I will put the game in a box and send it to him.

Thane will like my note.

He will like the game.

The Scribe

The scribe sat on a bench.

His long robe was made of cloth.

He wrote as God spoke to him.

He wrote on a scroll.

The pen with which he wrote was a quill.

The man wrote and wrote.

I am glad that the scribe wrote on the scroll as God spoke to him.

God chose this scribe to write of Him.

Ten Dimes

Ike has ten dimes.

He plans to give a dime to God.

Ike thinks it is right and wise to give a tenth to God.

Ike will go to the store with the nine dimes that he has left.

He will spend five of his dimes at the store.

Then he will save the rest of his dimes in his bank at home.

It is wise to save some of the dimes.

Can we tell why?

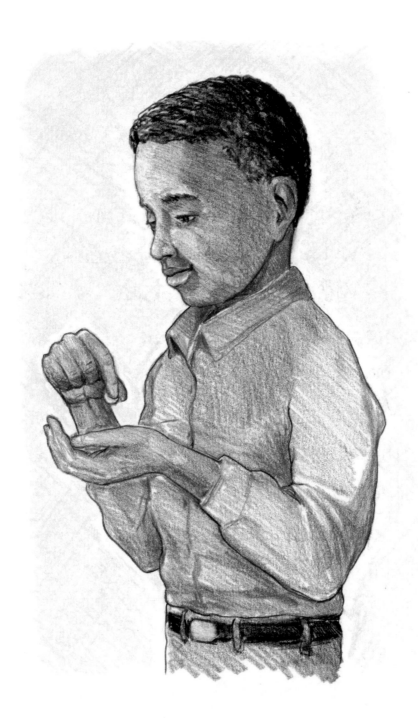

On the Line

Mom will hang the wash on the line.

She will hang a dress and a robe.

She will hang the dish cloth.

She will hang Dad's pants.

The white socks will be on the line.

My pink cape will be on the line.

The brisk wind will whip at the wash.

The hot sun will help dry the wash.

Then Mom will take the things from the line.

Next she will hang the nice drapes on
the line.

The wind will whip the dust from
the drapes.

The drapes will have a fresh smell.

Dale on His Trike

Dale is not big in size, but he has a big trike which he likes to ride.

Dale will ride his trike on the path.

He will ride to the pond.

He will sit on his trike on the bank of the pond.

Five ducks swim on the pond.

Dale will toss crumbs to the ducks as he sits on his trike.

The ducks will swim to the edge of the pond to get the crumbs.

All five ducks will quack and quack.

Then Dale will ride his trike back on the path to his home.

He will wave to the ducks as he rides.

It Is a Gift!

Dad has a long box.

It is a gift.

Dad will lift the lid of the box.

The box has a white rose with a long stem.

It has a red rose with a long stem.

Mom chose the white rose.

I like the red rose best.

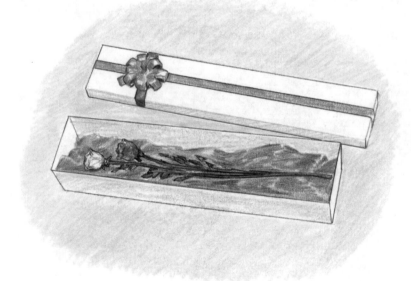

Dad will fill the vase.

Then Mom will place the white rose in the vase.

I will place my red rose in the vase.

My red rose will not wilt.

We think the gift from Dad is nice.

We will tell him, "Thanks!"

A Trip to the Store

Eve went to the store.

She rode on a bike.

Eve got grape jam.

She got five limes.

She got a bone for Dane.

Dane is Eve's big dog.

Eve will place the grape jam, the limes, and the bone in a tote bag on the side of the bike.

Then Eve will ride the bike home.

Big Dane will be glad to get his bone.

A Close Race

Mike and Jud will race.

The lads will stand on the white line.

When the gun bangs, then the lads will run.

The race will be close.

Mike will run fast.

Jud will run fast.

At last Mike hits the rope.

He will cross the white line.

Jud is close.

He will cross the white line next.

Mike wins the race!

The Class

The class will go on the stage.

The class will sing a song.

Next Gene will quote a page from the theme which he wrote.

The theme is quite nice.

The theme tells of God.

Then the class will sing a song of God's love.

Next the class will go from the stage.

The class will go from the stage in a nice line.

Miss Blake wants them to sit at the front.

The class did a fine job.

Five in a Hive

God tells the five to make a hive.

This hive will be the home of the five.

These will make haste to fly to the rose buds that God has made.

The five like the taste and will sip from the buds.

Then the five will not waste time but will fly home to the hive.

A Truce! A Truce!

A truce! A truce!

We call a truce

At the old, old spruce!

Be not so rude

And not so crude—

Just come to the truce

At the old, old spruce!

A Huge Black Mule

The huge mule is black.

We will climb up on his back.

We will pat him and hum a tune
to the mule.

We will be kind to the huge mule.

He will be kind to us.

A Cube

Dad will cut a cube from a spruce.

It will be a crude cube.

Then Dad will rub and sand the crude cube.

Dad did a fine job on the cube.

June will set the cube on the top shelf.

This will be a safe place.

The Tunes

Lynn will hum a tune.

The tune she hums is a cute tune.

Then she will pick up a flute to make a tune.

The tune on the flute will not be a long tune.

Lynn thinks it is fun to hum, but she likes to use the flute.

Fun on a Tube

Bruce has a tire tube.

He will use it while he swims.

Bruce will not be rude with his
tire tube.

He will be kind.

He will let Luke use his tube.

Bruce and Luke think the tire tube
will be fun.

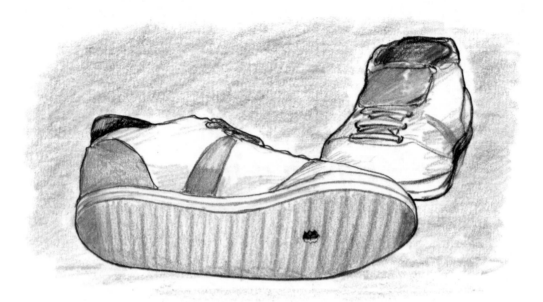

A Hole in a Sole

When did Steve get a hole in his sole?

He is not sure.

The hole is not big, but a stick got stuck
in the hole.

Then a rock got stuck in the hole.

Steve must go to the shop and let the
man fix the hole in his sole.

Bruce on a Mule

Bruce sat on a mule.

The mule is huge, but he is tame.

He has a black mane.

Bruce is kind to the mule.

The mule lets Bruce ride on his back.

The Huge Whale

The whale is huge.

He likes to swim.

He swims fast.

He is not shy.

We like to watch the whale swim.

God made the huge whale.

A Stitch in Time Saves Nine!

"Why such a grim face?" Mom asks Ruth.

"I have a job to do and not much time to do it. I want to be wise in the use of my time," Ruth tells Mom.

"And what job is that?" asks Mom.

"Here is a small rip in my cape. The rip is less than an inch long. I think I can save a lot of time if I fix the rip while it is so small."

"What a wise lass!" Mom tells Ruth.

"This act will prove to us that a stitch in time saves nine!"

114

The Cold Drink

What will Madge do when it is hot, hot, hot?

She will fix cold drinks.

She will take ice from the pan.

Madge will place five ice cubes in Nan's glass.

She will place five ice cubes in Ted's glass.

The drink tastes fine.

Nan and Ted like the nice, cold drink.

The Tale of the Fox

Dad will tell us a tale.

This will be just a fun tale.

Dad will tell us a tale of a fox that was tame.

This pet fox ate strange things.

He ate nuts, grapes, rice, and figs.

At times the fox ate ice cubes.

Such strange things this fox ate.

He was quite a pet!

Wade's Ice Cubes

Wade made ice cubes.

He will use them in his glass.

He is sure that the ice cubes will make his drink cold.

But Wade left the cubes in the hot sun.

Wade is quite sad.

He will not get a cold drink.

Can we tell why?

Did the hot sun melt the ice cubes?

The Pane

Dave broke the pane with a big rock.

The rock made a huge hole.

Dave felt bad.

Dad told Dave that he must fix the pane.

Will it cost Dave a lot to fix the pane?

Watch Luke!

Watch Luke jump.

He will try to jump the fence.

Did he make it?

Yes, he made it!

Watch Luke run.

He will run to the lake.

He will get a drink at the lake.

Then he will run home.

He will sit by the gate.

Luke must rest.

Luke will doze by the gate.

The Cute Pup

Duke is a pup.

He is a cute pup, but his legs will not help him run fast.

Can we tell why?

He is black with a white spot on his neck and left side.

Duke likes to drink milk and munch on his bone while he rests next to the fire.

The Ninth Grade

My sis is in ninth grade.

She likes the math class best.

When the bell rings, Sis has lunch.

Then she must write. She will use a pad to take notes.

She will write big sums on the note pad.

She must use rules so that the sums will be right.

Sis likes ninth grade math.

The Yule Log

The yule log is big.

It will make a big blaze.

The yule log rests on the grate.

Dad sits by the fire to watch.

He tells Pete and Jane of Christ as
a Babe.

Dad, Pete, and Jane will have a nice
time by the fire.

127

Steve

Steve is mute.

He cannot tell his name as we can.

He cannot sing as we sing.

But Steve can use his hands to sing and to tell us things.

Steve is nice.

We will not make fun of Steve.

We will be kind to him.

God has made Steve as he is.

God loves Steve just as much as He loves us.

The Bride

Kate will dress like a bride, but she is just nine.

She has put on a white dress with lots of lace on it. She holds a bunch of pink rose buds and smiles as she acts like a bride.

Dad tells Kate, "Have fun, but much time must pass till I can give my last to be a bride."

The Lime Drink

Mom has a sack of limes which she got at the store.

She will use the limes to make a cold drink.

She will cut them with a knife.

Then she will make lots of lime drink.

When Dad and Tate come home, the drink will taste fine to them.

132

A Trip to the Lake

Dad and James will go to the lake to fish.

James hopes to catch lots of fish to take home.

He will sit on the bank and cast his line into the lake.

Dad will wade into the lake.

He will use his net to catch fish.

The Ox and His Mate

The ox will graze on the grass.

The ox is huge.

The ox is strong.

The man will use this ox to help lift the log from the mire.

He will yoke this ox with his mate.

Then both will drag the log from the mire.

135

Jake Will Make a Lake

Jake is in the sand pile.

He has his huge crane with him.

He will use his crane to make a lake in the sand pile.

Jake's crane will make a wide hole in the sand.

Jake will have a fine time with his crane in the sand pile.

Quite a Sight!

Mom has on a hat with a big brim.

The hat has a big plume on it.

Mom has on a long dress with a jade pin at the neck.

The jade stone will shine when the light hits it.

Mom has a stole made of fox.

Mom is quite a sight.

I think she will win the prize.

Help! Help!

Help! Help!
I fell from the swing.
I cut my chin.
Dad ran to me.
He will fix me up.
Dad will take me home.
He will wrap ice cubes in a cloth.
He will place a cold cloth on my chin.
Then I will rest on my bed.

141

Frank's Lunch

Mom will pack a lunch.

She will use a big bag.

She will put ham, cake, dates, and grapes in the bag.

She will hand the bag to Frank.

He will take the bag to class with him.

At lunch time, he will take the ham, cake, dates, and grapes from the bag.

Frank likes his lunch.

Frank thinks, "Mom made me a fine lunch."

He will be sure to thank Mom when he gets home.

Rice and Grapes

Mom sent Meg to the store.

She got nine sacks of grapes.

She got rice from the top shelf.

Meg will help Mom fix the rice.

Mom will use the grapes to make jam.

She will make the jam on the stove.

Meg likes grape jam.

She will slice a bun.

She will put the grape jam on a bun.

Meg will take a huge bite!

M–m–m–m!

Such fine jam Meg ate.

A Nice Ride

Come take a ride with us.

We will go at five.

Do not be late.

We will go up, up, up.

We will go up fast.

This will be a nice ride.

We will smile as we take this ride.

Then we will take a dive.

The ride was not long.

But it was a fine ride.

The ride was in a plane.

The plane was not big.

We went nine miles on the ride.

On the next trip, we will go to the
next state.

We will go on a huge plane.

That ride will be long.

We will have a nice time.

The Ape

The ape sits in a cage.

His name is Pete.

He likes grapes.

He likes nuts.

He likes to swing.

The swing hangs from ropes.

Pete thinks it is fun to swing and swing.

Five Rules

Stan wrote these five rules on his slate.

Rules

1. I will do my chores well.
2. I will take pride in my job.
3. I will not waste time.
4. I will not take a bribe.
5. I will not gripe.

These rules will help Stan all of his life.

What Time Is It?

Ring! Ring! The clock wakes Wade.
What time is it? Wade will gaze at the
clock. Can he tell what time it is? Yes, the
clock tells him it is six.

Wade jumps from his bed. He lifts the shade. The sun is up. He runs to take a quick bath. Then he must dress fast.

Dad and Wade plan to take a long trip to the lake. Wade must not be late. He is glad to have a clock to tell him the right time!

Can We Find the Sum?

Miss Chase will tell the class to find the sum. She will tell the rule. Then she will ask the class to write the rule on the note pads.

Mike Drake likes the rule. It will help him do these sums.

Here is what Mike and the class wrote:

Add six plus five.	6	5
Add five plus six.	+5	+6
The sum is just the same.		

Add ten plus six.	10	6
Add six plus ten.	+6	+10
The sum is the same.		

Add five plus nine.	5	9
Add nine plus five.	+9	+5
The sum is the same.		

Can we tell what the rule is?

Which Size Is Best?

Lane is just a lad of six, but he is big. Dad wants to get Lane some pants at the store. Which size is best? Can Lane tell Dad the right size? Is it a size six?

Lane must try on the pants. The man at the store will tell Dad that a size six will not fit. Lane thinks a size nine is best. The man tells Lane that a size nine will be just fine.

Dad is glad. He gives a check to the man. The man puts Lane's pants in a sack, and Lane takes them home. Lane likes the pants and tells his dad, "Thanks."

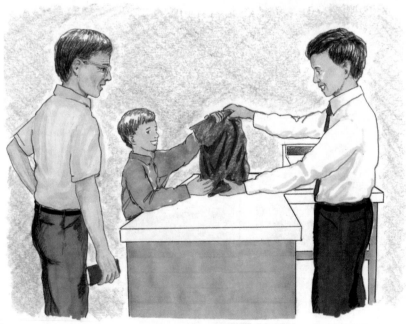

Bruce Has Six Rules

Bruce wrote six rules. He gave them to Dad. Dad thinks these rules will be fine if Bruce will live by them.

Rules

1. I must not fume.
2. I will not be rude.
3. I will not be crude.
4. I cannot hide my sin from God.
5. I must hate sin as God hates it.
6. A stitch in time saves nine.

Bruce hopes, with God's help, to live by these rules. Bruce wants to be a fine man who lives right.

The Kites

The phone rings. Pete runs to the phone.
It is his pal, Blake, on the line. Blake wants
Pete to go to the kite race with him.

Both lads will fly kites at the race. Pete has a huge kite that he made. The kite has a face on it. A smile is on the face.

Blake has a kite that he made. His kite has a plump whale on it.

The brisk wind will whisk both kites high in the sky. The kites will glide and glide in the sky.

Which kite will win the race?

The Dike

The men made a huge, strong dike to hold back the waves from the Dutch land. The men did a fine job on the dike. The dike held fast as time went by. All the land was safe.

One fall eve just at dusk, a small lad comes past the dike. He thinks he is quite safe. He is sure that the dike will hold back the waves from his land.

All at once his gaze falls on a small hole in the dike. The lad runs fast to his home.

He and his dad then run to tell the men that a hole is in the dike.

The men rush to the dike to mend the hole.
It might take them all night to make the dike
safe. Lots of men come to help. The dike
must hold back the waves from the land to
make the Dutch homes safe.

The job is well done! The lad did a fine thing. The men thank the lad. The lad smiles. He is glad his land is safe once more.

Whose Glove Is This?

Mom had a sad face when Dad came in the front drive.

"What is wrong with my wife?" spoke Dad in a kind tone. "Is the pup lost this time?"

"No, the pup is at home, but I have lost my left white glove. I think it fell from my lap when I got off the bus," Mom told Dad. "It is such a trite thing, but I wish I had put my name in the glove," spoke Mom in that same tone.

"Do not take so much blame," Dad spoke. "Why not ask God to help us find it? He must want to tell us a place to check. I will ask Him."

Just then Dave rode up fast on his bike.
"What have we here? Why the sad
face, Mom?"

Dad spoke with a smile and a wink at
Dave. "Mom has not lost all the cash, just
one white glove."

"Whose glove is this?" spoke Dave as he
slid the glove from his bag. "I rode my bike
from the store. This white glove was on the
grass by the bus stop just a half mile from
home. It must be Mom's glove."

"It is! It is! We must thank God!" Mom
told them. "It was not lost a long time, was
it? And it was so close to home all the time!"